KINDERGARTEN LEARN-TO-READ WORKBOOK

TRACE AND WRITE-YOUR-OWN SIGHT WORDS FOR BOOKS 1, 2 & 3!

Erika Burton, BSW

HALV ROUNDTABLE LEARNING

Name:_____

Date: _____

KINDERGARTEN LEARN-TO-READ WORKBOOK

CREATED BY HALV ROUNDTABLE LEARNING 2025

Name:_____

Date: _____

Copyright © 2025 by Erika Burton

All rights reserved. No part of this book may be reproduced in any manner whatsoever without written permission except in the case of personal, single-family use.

First Printing, 2025.

CREATED BY HALV ROUNDTABLE LEARNING 2025

Name:_____

Date: _____

Kindergarten Sight Words #1

Instructions: Practice writing the sight words on the lines.

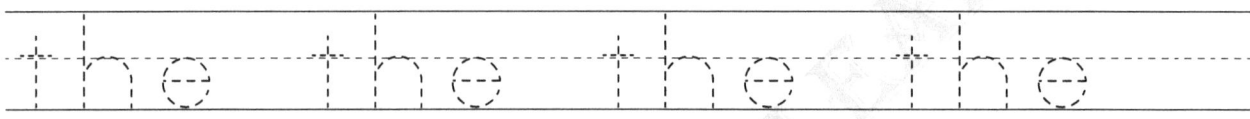

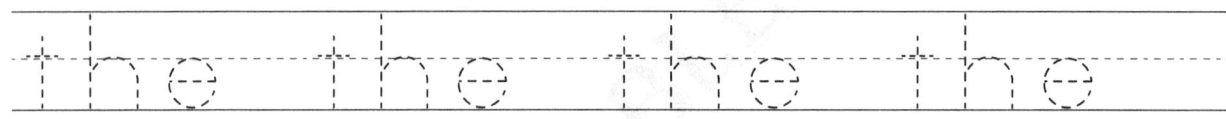

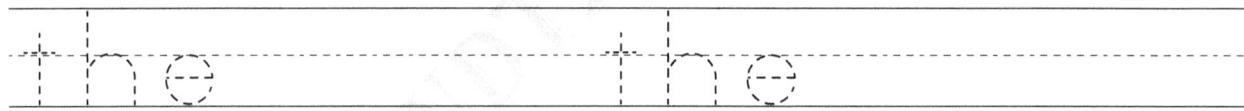

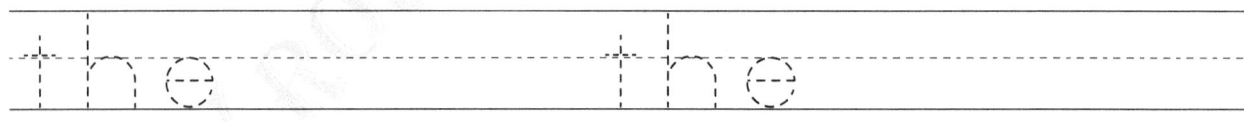

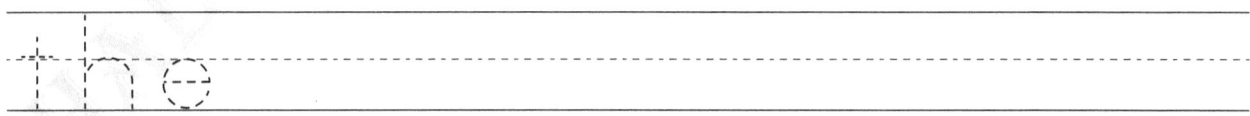

CREATED BY HALV ROUNDTABLE LEARNING 2025

Name:_____

Date: _____

Kindergarten Sight Words #2

Instructions: Trace and write the sight words on your own on the lines below.

this this this this

this this this this

this   this

this   this

this

this

CREATED BY HALV ROUNDTABLE LEARNING 2025

Name:_____

Date: _____

Kindergarten Sight Words #3

Instructions: Trace and write the sight words on your own on the lines below.

CREATED BY HALV ROUNDTABLE LEARNING 2025

Name:_____

Date: _____

Kindergarten Sight Words #4

Instructions: Practice writing the sight words on the lines.

a

a a a a a a a a

a a a a a a a a

a   a   a   a

a   a   a   a

a

a

CREATED BY HALV ROUNDTABLE LEARNING 2025

Name:_____

Date: _____

Kindergarten Sight Words #5

Instructions: Practice writing the sight words on the lines.

CREATED BY HALV ROUNDTABLE LEARNING 2025

Name:_____

Date: _____

Kindergarten Sight Words #6

Instructions: Trace the sight words and then practice writing on your own.

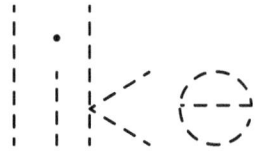

like like like like

like like like like

like   like

like   like

like

like

CREATED BY HALV ROUNDTABLE LEARNING 2025

Name:_____

Date: _____

Kindergarten Sight Words #7

Instructions: Trace the sight words and then practice writing on your own.

here here here

here here here

here   here

here   here

here

here

CREATED BY HALV ROUNDTABLE LEARNING 2025

Name:_____

Date: _____

Kindergarten Sight Words #8

Instructions: Trace the sight words and then practice writing on your own.

CREATED BY HALV ROUNDTABLE LEARNING 2025

Name:_____

Date: _____

Kindergarten Sight Words #9

Instructions: Trace the sight words and then practice writing on your own.

CREATED BY HALV ROUNDTABLE LEARNING 2025

Name:_____

Date: _____

Kindergarten Sight Words #10

Instructions: Trace the sight words and then practice writing on your own.

some

some some some

some some some

some   some

some   some

some

some

CREATED BY HALV ROUNDTABLE LEARNING 2025

Name:_____

Date: _____

Kindergarten Sight Words #11

Instructions: Trace the sight words and then practice writing on your own.

many

many   many   many

many   many   many

many   many

many   many

many

many

CREATED BY HALV ROUNDTABLE LEARNING 2025

Name:_____

Date:_____

Kindergarten Sight Words #12

Instructions: Trace the sight words and then practice writing on your own.

CREATED BY HALV ROUNDTABLE LEARNING 2025

Name:_____

Date: _____

Kindergarten Sight Words #13

Instructions: Trace the sight words and then practice writing on your own.

there there there

there there there

there   there

there   there

there

there

CREATED BY HALV ROUNDTABLE LEARNING 2025

Name:_____

Date: _____

Kindergarten Sight Words #14

Instructions: Trace the sight words and then practice writing on your own.

not not not not

not not not not

not   not

not   not

not

not

CREATED BY HALV ROUNDTABLE LEARNING 2025

Name:_____

Date: _____

Kindergarten Sight Words #15

Instructions: Trace the sight words and then practice writing on your own.

does   does   does

does   does   does

does   does

does   does

does

does

CREATED BY HALV ROUNDTABLE LEARNING 2025

Name:_____

Date:_____

Kindergarten Sight Words #16

Instructions: Trace the sight words and then practice writing on your own.

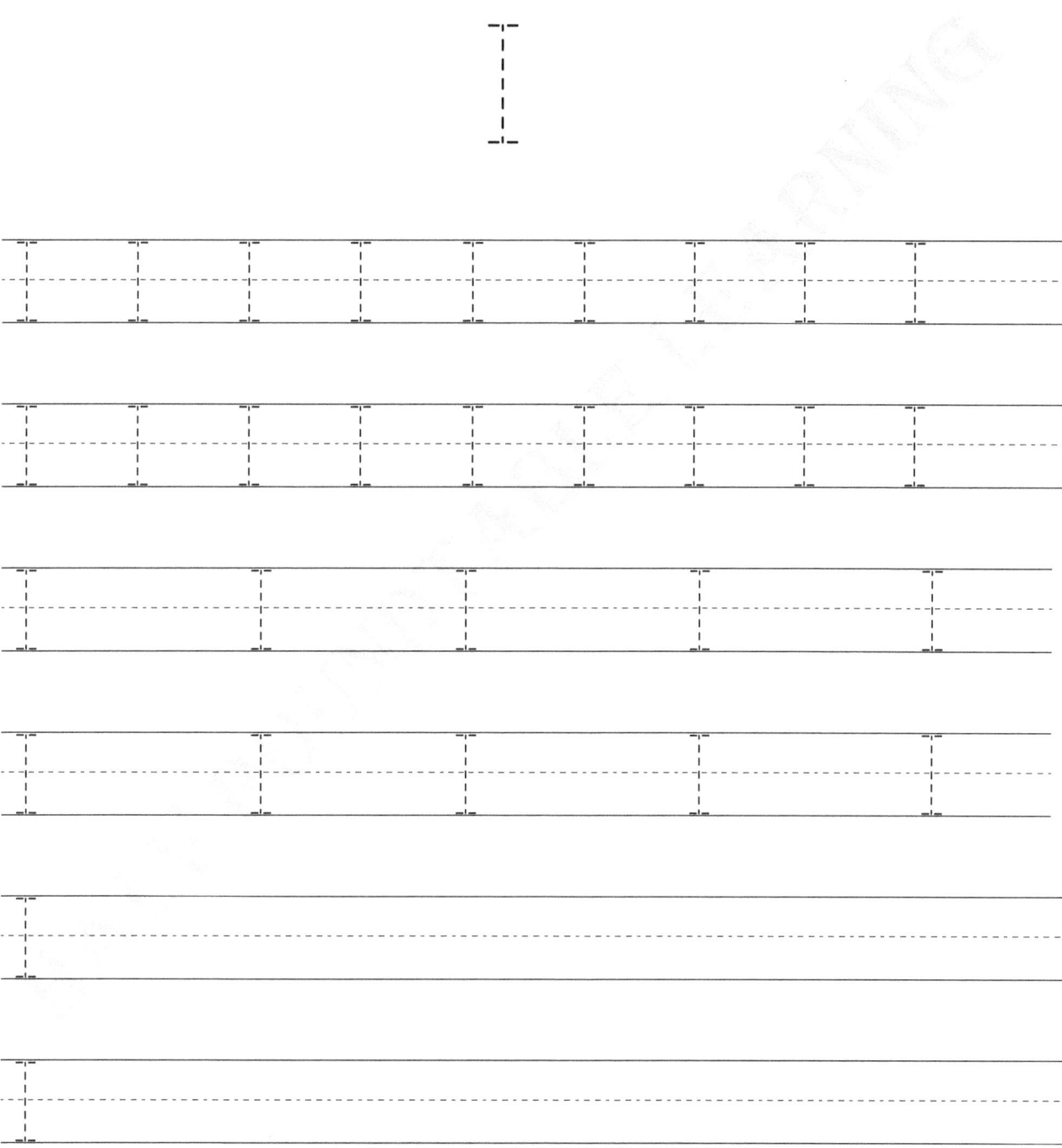

CREATED BY HALV ROUNDTABLE LEARNING 2025

Name:_____

Date: _____

Kindergarten Sight Words #17

Instructions: Trace the sight words and then practice writing on your own.

you

you you you you

you you you you

you   you

you   you

you

you

CREATED BY HALV ROUNDTABLE LEARNING 2025

Name:_____

Date: _____

Kindergarten Sight Words #18

Instructions: Trace the sight words and then practice writing on your own.

hi

hi hi hi hi hi hi

hi hi hi hi hi hi

hi hi hi

hi hi hi

hi

hi

CREATED BY HALV ROUNDTABLE LEARNING 2025

Name:_____

Date: _____

Kindergarten Sight Words #19

Instructions: Trace the sight words and then practice writing on your own.

my

my my my my my

my my my my my

my   my   my

my   my   my

my

my

CREATED BY HALV ROUNDTABLE LEARNING 2025

Name:_____

Date: _____

Kindergarten Sight Words #20

Instructions: Trace the sight words and then practice writing on your own.

name

name name name

name name name

name   name

name   name

name

name

CREATED BY HALV ROUNDTABLE LEARNING 2025

Name:_____

Date: _____

Kindergarten Sight Words #21

Instructions: Trace the sight words and then practice writing on your own.

CREATED BY HALV ROUNDTABLE LEARNING 2025

Name:_____

Date:_____

Kindergarten Sight Words #22

Instructions: Trace the sight words and then practice writing on your own.

in

in   in   in   in   in   in

in   in   in   in   in   in

in   in   in

in   in   in

in

in

CREATED BY HALV ROUNDTABLE LEARNING 2025

Name:_____

Date: _____

Kindergarten Sight Words #23

Instructions: Trace the sight words and then practice writing on your own.

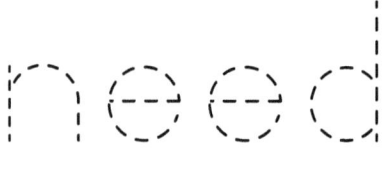

need   need   need

need   need   need

need   need

need   need

need

need

CREATED BY HALV ROUNDTABLE LEARNING 2025

Name:_____

Date: _____

Kindergarten Sight Words #24

Instructions: Trace the sight words and then practice writing on your own.

look

look look look

look look look

look   look

look   look

look

look

CREATED BY HALV ROUNDTABLE LEARNING 2025

Name:_____

Date: _____

Kindergarten Sight Words #25

Instructions: Trace the sight words and then practice writing on your own.

CREATED BY HALV ROUNDTABLE LEARNING 2025

Name:_____

Date: _____

Kindergarten Sight Words #26

Instructions: Trace the sight words and then practice writing on your own.

has

has   has   has   has

has   has   has   has

has   has

has   has

has

has

CREATED BY HALV ROUNDTABLE LEARNING 2025

Name:_____

Date: _____

Kindergarten Sight Words #27

Instructions: Trace the sight words and then practice writing on your own.

eats eats eats

eats eats eats

eats   eats

eats   eats

eats

eats

CREATED BY HALV ROUNDTABLE LEARNING 2025

Name:_____

Date: _____

Kindergarten Sight Words #28

Instructions: Trace the sight words and then practice writing on your own.

CREATED BY HALV ROUNDTABLE LEARNING 2025

Name:_____

Date: _____

Kindergarten Sight Words #29

Instructions: Trace the sight words and then practice writing on your own.

about about about

about about about

about   about

about   about

about

about

CREATED BY HALV ROUNDTABLE LEARNING 2025

Name:_____

Date: _____

Kindergarten Sight Words #30

Instructions: Trace the sight words and then practice writing on your own.

CREATED BY HALV ROUNDTABLE LEARNING 2025

Name:_____

Date: _____

Kindergarten Sight Words #31

Instructions: Trace the sight words and then practice writing on your own.

many

many   many   many

many   many   many

many   many

many   many

many

many

CREATED BY HALV ROUNDTABLE LEARNING 2025

Name:______________________

Date: ______________________

Kindergarten Sight Words #32

Instructions: Trace the sight words and then practice writing on your own.

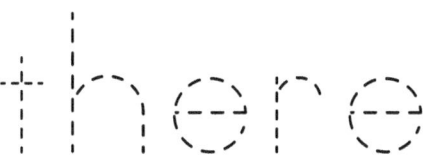

there

there there there

there there there

there there

there there

there

there

Name:_____

Date: _____

Kindergarten Sight Words #33

Instructions: Trace the sight words and then practice writing on your own.

see

see see see see

see see see see

see   see

see   see

see

see

CREATED BY HALV ROUNDTABLE LEARNING 2025

Name:_____

Date: _____

Kindergarten Sight Words #34

Instructions: Trace the sight words and then practice writing on your own.

Name:_____

Date: _____

Kindergarten Sight Words #35

Instructions: Trace the sight words and then practice writing on your own.

have have have

have have have

have   have

have   have

have

have

CREATED BY HALV ROUNDTABLE LEARNING 2025

Name:_____

Date: _____

Kindergarten Sight Words #36

Instructions: Trace the sight words and then practice writing on your own.

CREATED BY HALV ROUNDTABLE LEARNING 2025

Name:_____

Date: _____

Kindergarten Sight Words #37

Instructions: Trace the sight words and then practice writing on your own.

more

more   more   more

more   more

more   more

more

more

more

CREATED BY HALV ROUNDTABLE LEARNING 2025

Name:_____

Date: _____

Kindergarten Sight Words #38

Instructions: Trace the sight words and then practice writing on your own.

plus

plus plus plus plus

plus plus plus plus

plus   plus

plus   plus

plus

plus

CREATED BY HALV ROUNDTABLE LEARNING 2025

Name:_____

Date: _____

Kindergarten Sight Words #39

Instructions: Trace the sight words and then practice writing on your own.

equals

equals equals

equals equals

equals

equals

equals

equals

CREATED BY HALV ROUNDTABLE LEARNING 2025

Name:_____

Date: _____

Kindergarten Sight Words #40

Instructions: Trace the sight words and then practice writing on your own.

altogether

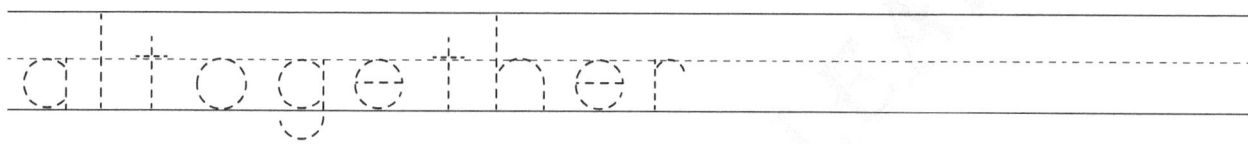

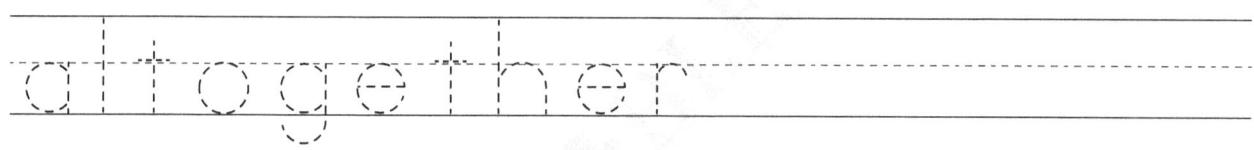

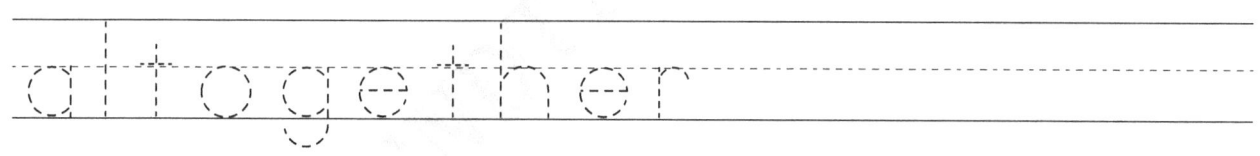

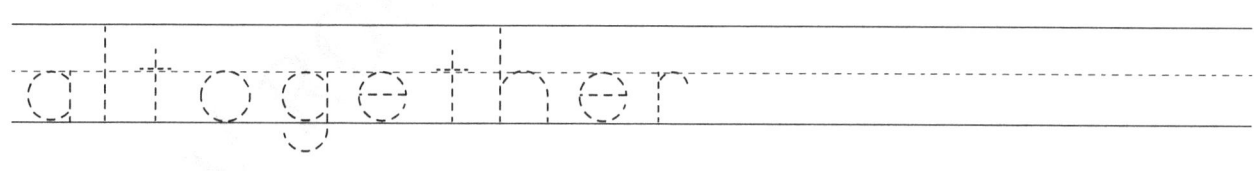

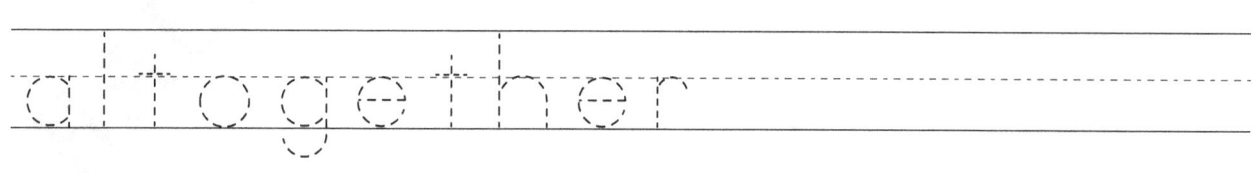

CREATED BY HALV ROUNDTABLE LEARNING 2025

Name:_____

Date: _____

Kindergarten Sight Words – Number One (1)

Instructions: Trace the sight words and then practice writing them on your own in the spaces.

1 one 1

one one one one

one one one one

one one

one one

one

one

Name:_____

Date: _____

Kindergarten Sight Words – Number Two (2)

Instructions: Trace the sight words and then practice writing them on your own in the spaces.

2   two   2

two two two two

two two two two

two   two

two   two

two

two

CREATED BY HALV ROUNDTABLE LEARNING 2025

Name:_____

Date: _____

Kindergarten Sight Words – Number Three (3)

Instructions: Trace the sight words and then practice writing them on your own in the spaces.

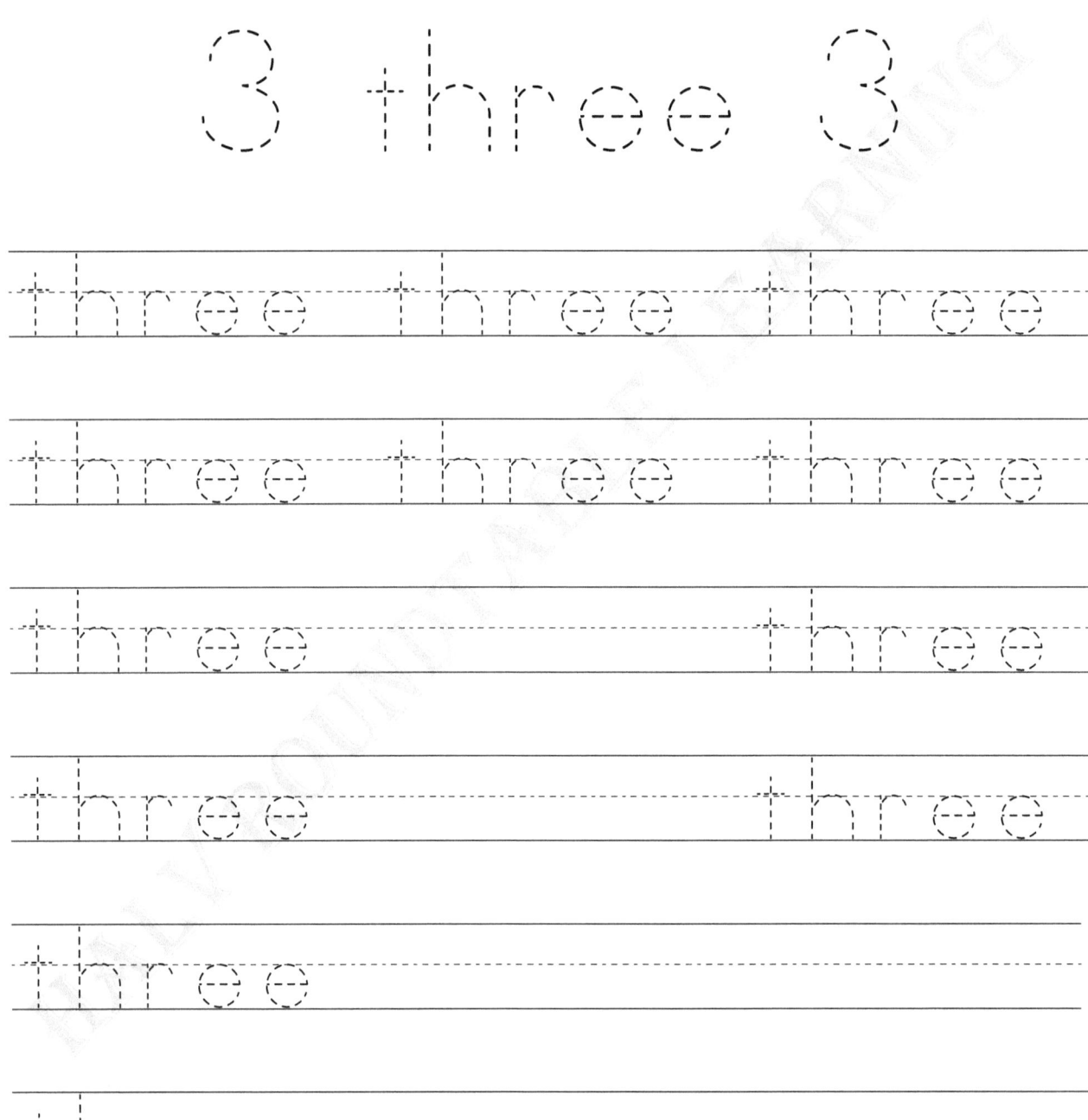

CREATED BY HALV ROUNDTABLE LEARNING 2025

Name:_____

Date: _____

Kindergarten Sight Words – Number Four (4)

Instructions: Trace the sight words and then practice writing them on your own in the spaces.

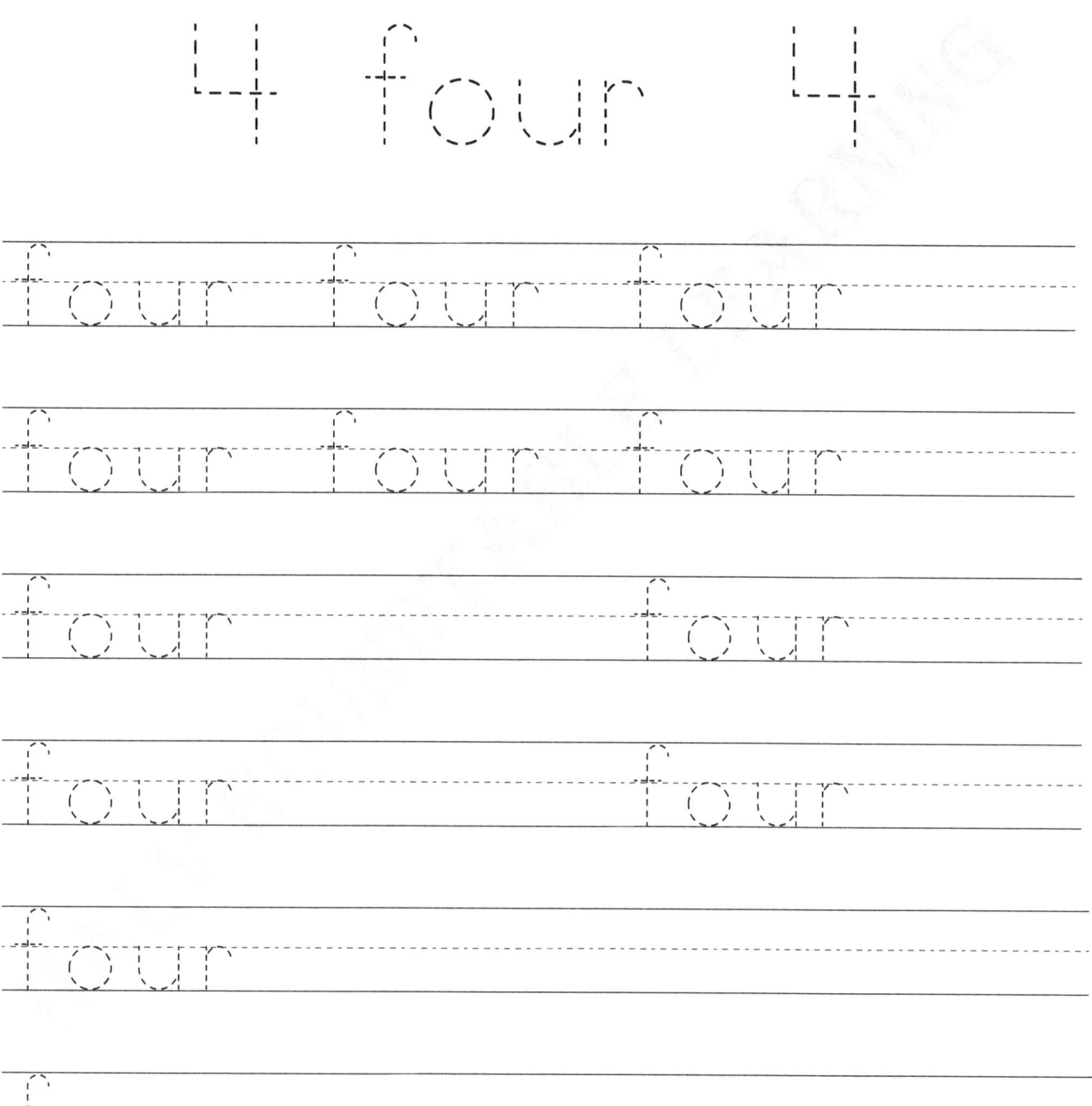

CREATED BY HALV ROUNDTABLE LEARNING 2025

Name:_____

Date: _____

Kindergarten Sight Words – Number Five (5)

Instructions: Trace the sight words and then practice writing them on your own in the spaces.

CREATED BY HALV ROUNDTABLE LEARNING 2025

Name:_____

Date: _____

Kindergarten Sight Words – Number Six (6)

Instructions: Trace the sight words and then practice writing them on your own in the spaces.

CREATED BY HALV ROUNDTABLE LEARNING 2025

Name:_____

Date: _____

Kindergarten Sight Words – Number Seven (7)

Instructions: Trace the sight words and then practice writing them on your own in the spaces.

7 seven 7

seven seven seven

seven seven seven

seven   seven

seven   seven

seven

seven

CREATED BY HALV ROUNDTABLE LEARNING 2025

Name:_____

Date: _____

Kindergarten Sight Words – Number Eight (8)

Instructions: Trace the sight words and then practice writing them on your own in the spaces.

CREATED BY HALV ROUNDTABLE LEARNING 2025

Name:_____

Date: _____

Kindergarten Sight Words – Number Nine (9)

Instructions: Trace the sight words and then practice writing them on your own in the spaces.

9 nine 9

nine nine nine

nine nine nine

nine   nine

nine   nine

nine

nine

CREATED BY HALV ROUNDTABLE LEARNING 2025

Name:_____

Date: _____

Kindergarten Sight Words – Number Ten (10)

Instructions: Trace the sight words and then practice writing them on your own in the spaces.

CREATED BY HALV ROUNDTABLE LEARNING 2025

Name:_____

Date: _____

Kindergarten Sight Words – Number Zero (0)

Instructions: Trace the sight words and then practice writing them on your own in the spaces.

0   zero   0

zero   zero   zero

zero   zero   zero

zero   zero

zero   zero

zero

zero

CREATED BY HALV ROUNDTABLE LEARNING 2025

Name:_____

Date: _____

Kindergarten Sight Words – Colors – Black

Instructions: Trace the sight words and then practice writing on your own.

black black black

black black black

black

black

black

black

CREATED BY HALV ROUNDTABLE LEARNING 2025

Name:_____

Date: _____

Kindergarten Sight Words – Colors -- Blue

Instructions: Trace the sight words and then practice writing on your own.

CREATED BY HALV ROUNDTABLE LEARNING 2025

Name:_____

Date: _____

Kindergarten Sight Words – Colors -- Brown

Instructions: Trace the sight words and then practice writing on your own.

CREATED BY HALV ROUNDTABLE LEARNING 2025

Name:_____

Date: _____

Kindergarten Sight Words – Colors -- Green

Instructions: Trace the sight words and then practice writing on your own.

CREATED BY HALV ROUNDTABLE LEARNING 2025

Name:_____

Date:_____

Kindergarten Sight Words – Colors -- Orange

Instructions: Trace the sight words and then practice writing on your own.

orange

orange   orange

orange   orange

orange   orange

orange

orange

orange

CREATED BY HALV ROUNDTABLE LEARNING 2025

Name:_____

Date: _____

Kindergarten Sight Words – Colors -- Pink

Instructions: Trace the sight words and then practice writing on your own.

CREATED BY HALV ROUNDTABLE LEARNING 2025

Name:_____

Date: _____

Kindergarten Sight Words – Colors -- Purple

Instructions: Trace the sight words and then practice writing on your own.

purple

purple   purple

purple   purple

purple

purple

purple

purple

CREATED BY HALV ROUNDTABLE LEARNING 2025

Name:_____

Date: _____

Kindergarten Sight Words – Colors -- Red

Instructions: Trace the sight words and then practice writing on your own.

CREATED BY HALV ROUNDTABLE LEARNING 2025

Name:_____

Date: _____

Kindergarten Sight Words – Colors -- Yellow

Instructions: Trace the sight words and then practice writing on your own.

www.ingramcontent.com/pod-product-compliance
Lightning Source LLC
Chambersburg PA
CBHW060539010526
44119CB00053B/763